Ritual Performance of Southeast Asia **Volume I**

Nora Ritual Performance of Southern Thailand
A Cross-Cultural Study

by

Cholthira Satyawadhna

CHOLTHIRA SATYAWADHNA

BA., MA. in Thai Language and Literature (Chula.)

Ph.D. in Anthropology (ANU.)

Cholthira Satyawadhna is a Thai anthropologist who has done tough fieldworks in Thailand, China, Malaysia and Indonesia. The focus of her anthropological research is on the marginal ethnic and cultural groups in Southeast Asia and the Thai-Yunnan periphery, hi-lights on women's role and status, gender studies, clan system and lineage, including the ethnohistory of the Tai and Southeast Asian peoples. Her deconstruction of the traditional capsuled knowledge of SEA has filled in the gaps and loop-holes of the Anthropology of SEA.

ANTHROPOLOGY OF SOUTHEAST ASIA

The Ritual Performance of SEA Series

The Ritual Performance of SEA Series shows the exposition of both rituals and dances of Southeast Asia in anthropological perspectives.

Volume I

Nora Ritual Performance of Southern Thailand
A Cross-Cultural Study

By Cholthira Satyawadhna

In this volume - Volume I, the researcher investigates Nora, a unique ritual performance of Southern Thailand and elaborates the belief system and social structure of the societies studied across the Southeast Asian border. It is discovered that this living culture has still woven the pride and virtue of the Southern Thai and the Siamese in Malaysia.

Copyright © 2014 by Cholthira Satyawadhna

Bangkok, THAILAND

ISBN-13: 978-1500901868 (CreateSpace-Assigned)

ISBN-10: 1500901865

BISAC: Social Science / Anthropology / Cultural

IMAGINATIVE SKETCH OF **NORA**

BY ANGKARN KALYANAPONGSA – POET LAUREATE OF SOUTHERN THAILAND

My Homage to Nora Gurus

Prelude

Nora (โนรา),[1] a Thai traditional local dance, is well-known as a performance genre that still survives and has a social function in Southern Thailand, notably in the three major provinces of Nakhon Si Thammarat, Songkhla, and Phatthalung. Most studies of the genre, either from an outsider-in or insider-out perspective, tend to perceive Nora as the pride of Southern Thais, preserved as the cultural heritage of the South.

My research goes beyond this stereotypical record of cultural heritage by focusing on the performers and trying to understand how they perceive Nora. I have spent almost three years studying Nora via several actual performances and have interpreted each one by reading in-between the lines. Space (stage and locality) and time (occasion and ceremonial rituals) have been taken into account. Apart from documents, archives, and fieldwork, I have also conducted action research among Nora dancers as individuals and a Nora troupe as a team. This research on Nora has been a delight. It has been fascinating to discover that there is a hidden structure within the Nora dance and ritual performance – unwritten knowledge and unsung wisdom, together with supernatural craftsmanship. The spirituality of Nora is thoroughly integrated into the dance performed, the poetry recited, the rites conducted, and the ritual space used. That is why Nora is and has been so enchanting, charming, and intriguing – truly a Pandora's Box for the explorer.

---

[1] Nora is an abbreviated form of *Manohra* (มโนหรา), a half-bird half-human character appearing in well-known Jataka story.

The significance of Nora as a ritual performance

I started my interest in Nora with wonder, further with pleasure, and later on, with curiosity. I found that, unlike the court dances of Central Siam like *Chui-chaay Brahmana* (ฉุยฉายพราหมณ์), where we appreciate the beauty, costume, and stylish conventional dance influenced by Brahmanism, the Nora performance has an extra value: a truly curative procedure of healing for all Nora dancers, performers, and members of Nora communities in Southern Thailand. It is a combination of artistic performance, plus ritualistic magic or shamanism,[2] and spiritual purification of all members in the Nora communities. Both physical and spiritual healings are part and parcel of the Nora ritual performance. A process of purifying "oneself" that takes place while dancing Nora or performing rituals is structurally deep-rooted within the Nora belief system. Therefore I perceive Nora as a living cultural survival of Southern Thailand.

Amid economic and social changes, Nora dance has become the pride of Southern Thai with a unique identity descended from countless community spiritual lineages of Nora. It is much more distinctive than the conventional Ayutthaya court dances and Bangkok traditional theatre which have lost any meaning and spiritual significance.

My research on Nora performance highlights the remaining legacies of the spiritual and cultural interchanges among the local communities of Southern Thailand. Along with other cultural expressions, the performing arts testify to the dynamic interaction of movement, sound and music, rhythm, and stories – stereotypes of plot and characters, but also intimate glimpses into people's hearts and spirits. From the viewpoint of the anthropology of religion, spirituality is the in-depth structure and function of Nora performance as its healing ritual is embedded into the communities' traditions, customary laws, values, and practices.

Nora as Art (*Silapa* ศิลปะ) and the identities of Nora dance

The Southern Thai Nora dance first inspired me with its elegant body movement which was both soft and strong in character, along with its musical accompaniment and singing by the key figures in the dance. Nora performances usually attract large and diverse local audiences. Although outside viewers including myself may not understand a word as the recital is in Southern Thai dialect, the lyrical words in beautiful rhymes,

---

[2] I prefer to use this term for the purpose of general understanding, another term – ritualist may be applicable in this context.

structured with patterns of lively rhythm, weave their magic. The most elegant and attractive gestures are the moving shoulders, arms, fingers and hands, all flying like birds in paradise, tempting audiences with styled gestures signifying deep meanings. Unlike the royal traditional dances in old Central Siam, Nora is not only a dance portraying a certain mythical story and expounding some noble precepts, but also a package of local wisdom that defies the passage of time.

I watched the Nora dance closely for the first time about three years ago in a welcoming ceremony at Walailak University[3] in Nakhon Si Thammarat Province in Upper Southern Thailand. This dance was a classical version from this part of the South, including the provinces of Phatthalung and Songkhla. It was also the first time I witnessed a dance where the key dancer led the rhythm of the drum in the orchestra. In this respect, Nora offers a contrast to classical Thai, modern and western dances. Although I could not understand the text as it was so fluent and rapid in Southern Thai dialect, I appreciated the beautiful rhyming verses, the melody, and the rise and fall in volume which hinted at the content.

Nora oral text is composed in verse known as *klon boraan,* กลอนโบราณ.[4] The verses flow in beautiful loosely-structured rhymes, within a lively rhythm. This example is the usual prelude[5] of a Nora performance:

ฤกษ์งามยามดี	ปานีชอบยามเพราะเวลา
ชอบฤกษ์ร้องเชิญ	ดำเนินราชครูถ้วนหน้า
ราชครูของน้อง	ลอยแล้วให้ล่องเข้ามา
มาอยู่เหนือเกล้าเกศา	มาอยู่เหนือเกล้าเหนือผม
มาช่วยคุ้มลมกันยา	กันทั้งลูกลมพรมโหวด
กันทั้งผีโภตมายา	มากันพรายแกมยา

---

[3] As Dean of the School of Liberal Arts at Walailak University during 2010-2013, I started research on Nora in 2010, first on my own, later in 2011-2012 as action research with my students who were Nora dancers, and finally with Kanit Sripaoraya, a PhD student in Asian Studies. Kanit has expanded the scope of her thesis from 'Barong Dance of Bali' to become in 2013 a comparative study of Barong, Nora and Mak-yong with fieldwork in the three areas of performance.

[4] Some may call this typical verse as *klon hok,* กลอนหก, but I prefer the term *klon boraan,* meaning 'archaic verse.'

[5] This is the first part of the invocation of the Nora Great Teachers, *Kham Kaat Khruu,* คำกาศครู, probably the most archaic of the versions I have found.

> This is a fine and auspicious time
> now the time is right,
> right to issue a call
> for the royal teachers to come forward,
> the royal teachers of ours, to float along here
> to be above our heads and pates, above our topknots, our hair
> to protect against wind, guard against medicine
> to guard against a wind-ball or Brahma's blast
> to guard against the spirits' lore,
> against the combination of spirits and medicine

The verbal text is quite difficult for an outsider to understand. It is a call to the Nora ancestral teachers, who are Rāja Gurus, ราชครู, "royal teachers," to come and witness the performance on such an auspicious day.

This vocabulary suggests that these Nora teachers were courtiers or had something to do with the court, yet Nora is quite a typical local performance. The verse invites the ancestral teachers to fly over the head, hair, topknots of the Nora disciples and to offer protection.

There are some phrases which are not easy to translate, like the call for the teachers to provide protection against a "wind ball," *luuk-lom* (ลูกลม), and "Brahma's blast" *phrom-woad* (พรมโหวด), perhaps a breezy blast (of wind). The last line begs the great teachers to protect them against two types of spirit, *phii phōt* (ผีโภต) and *(phii) phraay* (พราย), that have deceptive lore or magic, *māyā* (มายา), and also to guard them against "the combination of spirits and medicine," *phrai kaem yaa* (พรายแกมยา).

As Plato stated, *"Philosophy starts with wonder."*[6] Since this performance, Nora has been among my principal research project. I wondered what Nora is, why it has been so appreciated among the Southerners, where it originated, and how its system and structure function in Southern Thai communities.

---

[6] Plato's writings explored justice, beauty and equality, and also contained discussions on aesthetics, political philosophy, theology, cosmology, epistemology and the philosophy of language. These probably helped develop the foundation for Plato's study of metaphysics (the study of nature) and epistemology (the study of knowledge).

My Participatory action research on Nora performance

After readings up basic knowledge on Nora and making a number of field observations on typical Nora dances from some other provinces such as Songkhla and Patthalung, I decided to conduct a long-term participatory action research on Nora. My first move was to support the students of the School of Liberal Arts to establish the *Walailak University Nora Silapa-Sastra Club* in 2011, and help them to perform both "traditional" and "applied" Nora dances in public for various occasions.

For my study, I made a division of Nora into two parts: first, the knowledge or wisdom contained in the ritual aspect; and second, the performing arts including dance and drama. My research strategy was to conduct a micro study of the Walailak University Nora Silapa-Sastra Club within a macro framework of Nora as a cultural heritage of Southern Thailand, in order to understand the art and wisdom of the Nora culture from both the outsider-in and insider-out perspectives. The research was designed as a dynamic dialogue among three partners of at least three generations:

Generation A: Myself, an anthropologist from Bangkok who acted as an art director/producer of a few performances involving Nora dance performed by Southern Thais. During the three years (2011-2013) that I functioned as an art director, my students did not know that my involvement with Nora was research.[7]

Generation B: Kanit Sripaoraya (Kuck), a native Southern Thai by blood, who was grown up in Bangkok from childhood until graduating with a B.A. in Performing Arts from Bangkok University and an M.A. in Cultural Management from Thammasat University. She enrolled as a Ph.D. student in Asian Studies at Walailak University in 2011, while I was dean of the School of Liberal Arts, and chair of the doctoral program in Asian Studies (2010-2013). Kanit first submitted a proposal to work on the Barong Dance of Bali, Indonesia. She finished her coursework within one year, and took another year conducting anthropological fieldwork in Bali and Southern Thailand to compare Barong with Nora and Mak-yong[8]. She also co-directed with me three drama performances which featured Nora characters and dance, including drafting the script and performing as a dancer. The most recent, *"The Genesis of Nora"* was performed for audiences of over 1500 people at Thaiburi Theatre, some other performances held

---

[7] With this research plan, I could function as an outsider, a Bangkokian, and art appreciator, who was looking at Nora Dance seriously, supportively, and critically. I was critical of the students while they were dancing, practicing, and performing.

[8] *Mak-yong* is a Malay and Patani traditional dance for community healing. It has been promoted as part of Southeast Asia's cultural heritage by UNESCO.

at Wat Phra Mahathat, the principle temple of Nakhon Si Thammarat, and also among the ASEAN Cultural Shows at the International Conference on Asian Studies II at Walailak University on 18 February 2013.

Generation C: A group of my undergraduate students at the School of Liberal Arts who were Nora dancers, both professional and amateur. Among these, Ekachai Numsawat (Lek), a young professional dancer, was also a key informant. He has been a teacher on Nora for Kanit and other young dancers, not only at Walailak University, but also at some local schools in Songkhla, his hometown. He played lead roles in the plays directed by Kanit.[9]

Nora as Science (*Śāstra* ศาสตร์), knowledge and wisdom

Nora is not only an art but also a repository of knowledge and wisdom.

Nora ritual performance has been a truly 'curative' procedure for all Nora dancers and performers, past and present.

Unlike the texts recorded on palm-leaf manuscripts in Northern Thailand or Lanna, and Northeastern Thailand or Isan, Nora is mostly an oral tradition that has been passed on within various Southern Thai cultural groups obviously appeared in the lullabies (Prateep 2003: 4; 10-11). It consists of not only a mythical story which expounds some noble or royal precepts, but also a set of moral codes and ethical values of the Southern Thai clan system which are encoded in the dances and songs. Within each local community, Nora has a function to uphold the moral stance and ethical behavior of all community members.

Nora performers belong to a *Saay Nora* (สายโนรา), a Nora lineage. To be a Nora performer, and to achieve the status of a Nora teacher-adept (*khraub khruu nora*, ครอบครูโนรา), requires dedication to a "sacred" mission. The practitioners must abide by a strict code of conduct, including abstention from liquor, telling lies, cheating, or sexual abuse, and ideally should be single and always exhibit self-control. Those who achieve

---

[9] The relationship among the dancers and teachers was quite complex as Kanit was also a Teaching Assistant, and hence Ekachai was both her student but also her teacher on Nora. When they met, they would pay respect to each other with the gesture of *waai* (ไหว้). Actually Ekachai is the key insider for my research. Although he is more than willing to teach others the art of Nora, it took more than a year before he would pour out his wisdom of Nora for an outsider like myself, perhaps because of shyness, or because he would like to keep matters secret among his disciples. Thanks to Kanit for being a bridge into the secret and sacredness of Nora.

the status of a Nora teacher-adept gain esteem and authority. Through the power of knowledge with a sacred mission, the ancestral spirit of a Nora lineage may rule over not only his or her own lineage, but also some other more in the same clan.

There is a showcase at Ban Phru and Ban Klong Hwa, Songkhla, Anan, a male spirit-medium, well educated, was chosen by Khruu Hmoe Nora of his own lineage to control over two connected lineages, both of his paternal uncle and his maternal uncle, so he was possessed by *song chueak* (สองเชือก), or the 'two chains'.

Further on, it was realized that his maternal uncle, *Phii Chuad Bunkaew* (ผีชวดบุญแก้ว) who came to possess Anan, was a Great Nora Teacher, who was a representation of another six Nora chains, *hok chueak* (หกเชือก). This would resulted in Anan to become the medium for the eight teacher-adept ancestral spirits in care of the eight Nora lineages, *paet chueak* (แปดเชือก), within the same clan.

It is estimated that within the two provinces of Songkhla and Nakhon Si Thammarat, in the past fifty years until nowadays there have been more than hundred Nora lineages. (see Chatthip and Pornpilai 2541: 135-137)

According to the most recent fieldwork conducted by Ekachai at his father's hometown in June 2013, with the kind assistance of his father, eighteen Nora lineages together with eighteen teacher-adepts (ครูหมอโนรา) were found. The traditional Nora ritual is a purification of the soul that is significant for the well-being of the Nora communities. Some Nora dancers treat performance as a curative or purifying process for the self, or as a treatment for healing the sickness of another members of the Nora lineage.

Nora dance and Nora in the form of applied modern theatre art

The plays created for this project differed from traditional Nora performance. They were created in order to reconstruct a body of knowledge on the origins of Nora as perceived among the local communities of Southern Thailand. This perception differs from the account of Nora popularized by the court and generally upheld by Bangkok scholars.

In this latter view, Nora was invented in the Siamese court during the Ayutthaya period, but southerners believe that the Nora story originated in the area now called Phatthalung Province. They lay claim to Nora as a key part of the identity of Southern Thailand.

Nora costumes, including dress, ornaments and decorations, are all made with thousands and thousands of colorful beads. In my view, the culture of creating decorations with beads predated cloth weaving, and the woven patterns applied to cloth derived from the bead patterns. Nora is an archaic culture, a remnant of the long history of ethnical interactions among the Tai/Thai/Siamese and their Austroasiatic and Austronesian connections, with a strong influence from Brahmanism and Hinduism, and later mixed with Chinese beliefs.[10]

The scripts, choreography, and performing techniques for these novel plays were created on the basis of research among Nora dancers who were all of southern origin. In particular, the play *"The Genesis of Nora"* was scripted on the basis of documentary research cross-checked by field investigation and in-depth interviews with some Nora key performers from local communities in the three provinces.

The performances were greatly appreciated by both local audiences and government officials of the province. The performers were able to earn a little money donated by members of the audience. Within one academic year, our Nora troupe expanded from two to twelve dancers with many other members providing logistic and moral support.

Ekachai (Lek), our principal dancer, a freshman in political science, was born in Songkhla, without knowing that he was in a family associated with great Nora teacher-adept. He fell in love with Nora from childhood and practiced on his own Nora. His father, who was a motorcar-technician (ช่างยนตร์), was not supportive. Ekachai ran away to follow some Nora troupes and tried to find a master who would teach him to dance Nora properly. There is a Thai expression, *Khruu phak, lak jam* (ครูพัก ลักจำ), meaning *"when the teacher rests, the student learns in secret."* Ekachai learnt in this way until he could master the basics of Nora by himself and later was accepted by a local Nora teacher affiliated to the lineage of Khun Śri-Śraddhā, the most highly esteemed Nora lineage. When Ekachai entered high school, his father withdrew his objections as his son promised that he would pay full attention to his study in order to enter college. Ekachai kept his word and gained admission to the Walailak University political science program in 2011. Since then he has been active in promoting Nora by becoming a co-founder of the Silapa-Sastra Club and its first teacher.

---

[10] The great-grandparents of Ekachai who were affiliated with a Nora lineage were Chinese. The song for Nora dance that was first introduced to Walailak Nora troupe by Ekachai, our principal dancer, has a combination of Chinese melody with traditional Nora melodies.

Several other students, mostly female, were eager to learn and could learn fast. They were always willing to accept invitations to perform, no matter how far it was from Walailak University. At first, costumes were shared, but as the troupe became popular, most purchased a Nora bead-dress to fit their own body.

In the second year of our action research, Kanit and the Nora dancers were encouraged to stage a performance, integrating Nora dance into a play with script, plot, and characters adapted from a Thai literary classic, Phra Abhaimanī (พระอภัยมณี). This modern Thai opera named, Gīta-Nātakāra Duekdamban, คีตนาฏการดึกดำบรรพ์, "The Ancient Dance," was performed both at Walailak University and at the University of Hamburg, Germany, in May 2012, on the occasion of the 150th Anniversary of the German-Thai Diplomacy Relationships.

While the performance was a great success, I also learnt a lot from observing Ekachai. Before every performance, a Nora key dancer will recite a secret formula called Gāthā mahā saneha (คาถามหาเสน่ห์), "The great charm formula," to make himself or herself more attractive and win applause from the audience.

When donning the Nora costume consisting of several pieces of beadwork for the head, shoulders, breast, hips, legs, and toes, including necklaces, armbands, footbands, and ten sharp fingernails like birds, Nora dancers intone the Gāthā kan khii yiaw, คาถากันขี้เยี่ยว, "Formula to guard against urination and defecation," to avoid any embarrassment as they have to perform for hours.

Exactly when starting to perform, they secretly recite Gāthā kan saniad jañrai, คาถากันเสนียดจัญไร, "Formula to protect against evil-doing," to ward off any malign or malicious forces.

Kanit told me that the first two gāthā may be kept in writing but not the third which is considered especially secret as well as sacred. They believed they might be killed by rival clans if they do not preserve the secrecy. It appears that Nora shamans have formulas both for protecting themselves and for doing harm to others in order to prevent others doing harm to themselves. However, to avoid this matter, Ekachai allowed Kanit to write the "Formula to protect against evil-doing" on a small piece of paper which, after she had learned the formula by heart, she burnt. Other formulas were used for healing patients, people of the community, members of the Nora lineage, and for preventing evil spirits doing harm to them.

I witnessed a *Pithii yeap sen*, พิธีเหยียบเสน, the "treading-the-spirit rite," in which a ritual master, possessed by a Nora ancestral spirit, heals a baby. The *sen* is a red mark found on some part of the baby's body, usually the head, forehead or neck, believed to be the result of some harm done by an evil spirit (*sen* means spirit in Black Tai language). *Yeap* is a term used only for an action performed by the feet, the lowest part of the body, which usually should not be allowed to touch someone's head. Yet in this rite, the Nora ritual master touched the baby's head with a foot while reciting a formula in order to chase away the evil spirit and thus protect the baby. I believe this rite is part of the living cultural survivals of Southern Thailand, part of the typical clan belief systems of the Thai with Austroasiatic and/or Austronesian connections.

Kamneud Nora, กำเนิดโนรา: The genesis of Nora[11]

The myth of origin of Nora presented here is a popular version from Phatthalung Province as told by Khun U-Patham Narakorn, a highly respectful Nora master.

> Once upon a time, there was a king named *Phraya Saifa Fa Faat* (พระยาสายฟ้าฟาด, Lord of Lightning), who had a daughter named *Nang Nuan Thong Samli* (นางนวลทองสำลี, the princess who had a golden radiance and was soft like cotton). One day, the princess dreamed that a *deva* showed her the twelve poses of dancing with a specific collection of musical instruments, which was later known as Nora. Once awake, she practiced what had been shown to her, and this dance became popular in the palace.
>
> One day, she happened to have a desire to eat pollen from lotuses in the pond in front of the royal palace. She then became pregnant but continued to dance as ever. When the king-father saw her pregnant, he believed that she had committed an inauspicious act and banished her from the kingdom by putting her on a raft with about thirty courtiers.
>
> The princess' raft arrived at an island called Kashang (เกาะกะชัง) where she settled down and gave birth to a little prince, called *Kumāra Noy*. She trained her young son to dance Nora and he was very talented. When he grew up, the prince traveled on a merchant ship and showed Nora dance at every destination until he

---

[11] Co-translated with Dr. Wannasarn Noonsuk. There are other versions with differences of detail according to how the peoples of different places perceived the origin of Nora. Kanit Sripaoraya is further researching these myths in her doctoral research.

arrived at the kingdom of his grandfather. As people soon talked about his beautiful dancing, his grandfather secretly came to see him perform. As his dance was stunning and his face remarkably resembled that of his mother, the king summoned him and discovered that he was his grandson. The king then invited his daughter back to the kingdom and asked his grandson to dance for him once again. As a reward, he gave him the royal ornaments, which became the costume for all Nora dancers. The king then offered his grandson the title of *Khun Śrī Śraddhā*, who was revered as the Founder-Teacher of Nora, in other words, the Founder of a Nora clan and lineages.

While doing fieldwork and in-depth interviews, I found that there has been some social stratification and hierarchy within the "hidden structure" of Nora lineages. The Nora lineage of *Khun U-patham Nara*korn is closely affiliated to the artistic clan-line of Khun Śrī Śraddhā, the most highly respected in the Nora hierarchy (see Louis Dumont, *Homo hierarchicus* 1977; *Homo aequalis* 1991).

Although Khun Śrī Śraddhā was a man, the above myth of the genesis of Nora portrays the origin of Nora dance as a heavenly gift, imported via a woman, a royal princess (นางนวลทองสำลี). Her son, the young prince (กุมารน้อย), was trained to dance Nora by her, the "Mother" of Nora Dance.

Khun Śrī Śraddhā was awarded the royal ornaments which became the Nora costumes by his maternal grandfather, The Lord of Lightening (พระยาสายฟ้าฟาด), because he was direct heir of this royal blood-line. The inheritance was down through him because of his mother's status, not from any father(s) of unknown origin.

The annual gathering and invocation of the ancestors

Once a year, the members of a Nora clan with several lineages gather together for the *Pithī Nora long khruu* (พิธีโนราลงครู). At this gathering the senior member of the principal clan and the *Khruu hmoe Nora*, ครูหมอโนรา or Nora teacher-adept (who may be the same person) lead the ceremonies which last for three days and three nights among the Nora clans/lineages of Songkhla and Phatthalung, but nowadays are compressed into one day and one night in Nakhon Si Thammarat. (Chatthip and Pornpilai 2541: 132-137)

On the first day, the Nora teacher-adept performs a ceremony called *Kaat khruu* (กาศครู) at which all the *Taa Yaay Nora*, ตายายโนรา, the Nora ancestors of the long past, are invoked to bring prosperity and protection from maladies, vicious spirits, and bad luck for all their descendants. The invocation is in a poetic form (*klon boraan*), with versesconsisting of four hemistiches with four to six syllables per hemistich and an internal rhyme. A version of this extract invocation, believed to be the oldest, is as followed[12] :

The Invocation performed at the Kaat khruu Ceremony (พิธีกาศครูโนรา)

ฤกษ์งามยามดี ปานีชอบยามเพราะเวลา ชอบฤกษ์ร้องเชิญ ดำเนินราชครูถ้วนหน้า
ราชครูของน้อง ลอยแล้วให้ล่องเข้ามา มาอยู่เหนือเกล้าเกศา มาอยู่เหนือเกล้าเหนือผม
มาช่วยคุ้มลมกันยา กันทั้งลูกลมพรมโหวด กันทั้งผีโภตมายา มากันพรายแกมยา
ละมบเข้าฝังไว้ริมทาง มากันให้ถ้วนให้ถี่ มากันลูกนี้ทุกที่ย่าน ละมบเข้าฝังไว้ริมทาง
มากันลูกนี้ทุกที่ย่าน ละมบเข้าฝังไว้ริมทาง จำไว้แวะซ้ายแวะขวา สิบสองหัวช้างสิบสอง
หัวเชียก จำให้พ่อร้องเรียกหา ถ้าพ่อไม่มา ลูกยาจะได้เห็นหน้าใคร เห็นหน้าแต่ท่านผู้อื่น
ความชื่นลูกยามาแต่ไหน ให้ลูกเหลียวหน้าไปหาใคร เหมือนไยราชครูถ้วนหน้าฯ
ลูกไหว้ครูพักอีกทั้งครูสอน ไหว้แล้วเอื้อนกลอนต่อมา ไหว้ครูสังสอนข้า พ่อมาคุ้มหน้าคุ้ม
หลัง มาเถิดพ่อสายสมร มาคุ้มลูกเมือนอนเมือนัง มาคุ้มข้างหน้าข้างหลัง
พ่อมาวังซ้ายวังขวา ราชครูของน้อง ลอยแล้วให้ล่องเข้ามา ราชครูของข้า
ดำเนินเชิญมาให้หมดสิ้น ไหลแล้วให้เทกันเข้ามาฯ
ขุนโหรญาโหร ขุนพรานญาพราน โปรดปรานเหนือเกล้าเกศา ไหว้พรานเทพเดินดง
พระยาพรานคงเดินป่า พรานบุญพฤกษา เดินจำนำหน้าราชครู แม้นผิดแม้นพลาดตรง
ข้อไหน ท้าวไทยเมตตาได้เห็นดูฯ
บรรดาราชครู มาอยู่เบื้องซ้ายเบื้องขวา ลูกจับเริ่มเดิมมา ไหว้ขุนศรัทธาเป็นประธาน
ไหว้หลวงเสนได้เป็นครูพัก เป็นหลักนักเลงแต่โบราณ ถัดแต่นั้นทองกันดาร ไหว้ตา
หลวงเสนสองเมือง ไหว้ตาหลวงคงคอ ผมหมอไหว้ท้าววิจิตรเรือง โปรดให้รับท้าวเข้าสู่
เมือง ลือเลื่องความรู้ได้เล่าเรียน พ่อมาสอนศิษย์ไว้ต่างตัว พ่อไม่คิดกลัวเพราะความ
เพียร สิบนิ้วข้าหรือคือเทียน เสถียรสถิตยอไหว้ไปฯ
ยอไหว้พระยาโถมน้ำ โฉมงามพระยาลุยไฟ พระยาสายฟ้าฟาด ลูกน้อยนั่งร้องกาศไป
พระยามือเหล็กพระยามือไฟ ไหว้ใยตาหลวงคงคอ ไหว้ลูกของพ่อทีแทนมา
ชื่อจันทร์กระยาผมหมอ ตาหลวงคงคอ ผมหมอหลวงชมตาจิตร
เมื่อยามพ่อเป็นหลวงนาย แต่ท้าวมาไร้ความคิด หลวงชมตาจิตร

---

[12] I would like to thank Dr. Chris Baker and Prof.Dr. Pasuk Phongphaichit for their generous support in translating the ancient literary piece of the invocation for me. Other thanks go to Asst.Prof.Dr.Thanya Sangkhapandanond, Jen Songsomphan, Kanit Sripaoraya, and Ekachai Numsawat who helped me cross-check the text and interpret its meaning and possible implication.

ผิดด้วยสนมกรมชาววัง รับสั่งผูกคอให้ฆ่าเสีย พ่อไม่ทันได้สั่งลูก
บุญปลูกไม่ทันได้สั่งเมีย รับสั่งผูกคอให้ฆ่าเสีย ในฝั่งแม่น้ำย่านยาว
หากพ่อมาตายด้วยเจ็บไข้ ลูกรักจักได้ไปถามข่าว ในฝั่งแม่น้ำย่านยาว
ชีวิตพ่อม้วยมรณา ถ้าพ่อตายข้างฝ่ายบก ให้เป็นเหยื่อนกเหยื่อกา
พ่อไปตายฝ่ายเหนือ ให้น้ำเน่าน้ำเหงื่อไหลลงมา น้ำเน่าลายจันทร์
น้ำมันลูกลายแป้งทา โดกแข้งโดกขา ลูกยาไว้ทำไม้กลัดผม
ดวงเนตรพ่อทองผมสอด ลูกน้อยไว้ทำไม้หลอดอม ทำไม้กลัดผม
ชมต่างพ่อร้อยชั่งแก้ว โอ้พ่อร้อยชั่งแก้ว สองแถวพ่อร้อยชั่งอา
ร้อยชั่งรักข้า พ่ออย่าตัดรักเสียให้ม้วย พ่ออย่าตัดลูกเหมือนตัดตาล
พ่ออย่ารานเหมือนรานกล้วย พ่ออย่าตัดรัดเสียให้ม้วย
เอ็นดูด้วยช่วยรำโนห์ราฯ ...

* The principle of this translation is to keep the translation fairly literal, and put explanation in the notes.

This is a fine conjunction,[13] a good time now the time is right,

the right conjunction to issue a call

for all the royal teachers to come

the royal teachers of ours, to fly over and come down here

to come over our heads and pates, above our topknots, our hair

to protect against wind,[14] guard against medicine[15]

to guard against a twister[16] or Brahma's blast[17]

to guard against the spirits' trickery,

against the combination of spirits[18] and medicine

stop the hexing[19] buried beside the path

---

[13] ฤกษ์, *roek*, a time found by astrological reckoning, an auspicious time.

[14] Meaning evil forces or harmful charms that may be blown. This invocation would be used at contests where opponents might use supernatural devices.

[15] ยา, *ya*, like the medicine of Native Americans, meaning spiritual forces, here malicious.

[16] ลูกลม, *luk lom*, a windmill or similar device to stir the wind; perhaps malicious forces transmitted in the rivals' music, or blown in a pipe made of bamboo smeared with beeswax to make a loud vibration sound.

[17] พรมโหวด, *phrom wot*, the name of a formula to cause harm, usually instilled in cloth, but perhaps here in the music (see previous note).

[18] (ผี) พราย, *(phi) phrai*, Spirit of someone who died in water and who can act as carrier of a malicious charm.

[19] (ห) มบ, *mop*, malicious magic intended to kill, maim, or turn the victim mad.

protect us against all and every thing

come to protect us in every quarter stop

the hexing buried beside the path, remember,

come on the left and right

twelve elephant heads, twelve heads of the lineage[20]

remember fathers,[21] we call on you

if fathers do not come...

whose face shall we your children see? only the faces of others

where will your children find comfort?

who will you have us turn to?

the royal teachers are unlike any other

we pay respect to our models[22] and teachers

once done, then we intone verses

to pay respect to the teachers who taught us

fathers, come to protect us front and rear

do come, beloved fathers

come to protect us asleep or awake

come to protect us front and rear

fathers, come left, come right

royal teachers of ours, fly over and come down here

royal teachers of our, we invite every one of you

to come flooding in, pouring in

lord[23] astrologers, lord hunters

please come over our topknots

we honor the divine hunters traveling in the forest

the invulnerable lord hunters in the woods

the hunter Bun of the woods

who always walks before the royal teachers

if we have erred in any way

lords, please be merciful

---

[20] เชียก, *chiak*, form of เชือก, rope, meaning a line or lineage. There were 12 original "royal teachers" of Nora.

[21] Throughout, the caller addresses all the Nora teacher-adepts of the past as "fathers" and refers to he caller or all those calling as the "children", meaning descendants.

[22] ครูพัก, *khru phak*, a "passive teacher," one that the student imitates.

[23] ขุนโหรญาโหร, *khun hon ya hon*, where *khun* is a low noble title and *ya* means *okya* or *phraya*, one of the highest titles. The hunters have the same two titles.

all royal teachers, come to the left and the right
we start from the beginning
pay respect to Khun Sattha[24] who presides to Luang Sen,
a teacher we follow, as the principal artists[25] from ancient times
then pay respect to Thong Kandan
to Grandfather Luang Sen Song Mueang
to Grandfather Luang Khongkho the adept,[26]
pay respect to Lord Vijit Rueang,
we rejoice to welcome these lords into the city
the knowledge they have is famous
fathers, teach us to be like you
fathers, do not fear as we are diligent
our ten fingers are candles
constantly we bow to pay respect
to offer praise to Lord Thom Nam
the splendid Lord Fire-walker[27] , the Lord of Lightning
we children sit to sing our verses paying respect[28]
Lord Iron Hand, Lord Fire Hand,
we pay respect to Grandfather Luang Khongkho
to fathers' children who came in their place,
called Jankraya, the adept
Grandfather Luang Khongkho, the adept,
Luang Chom and Grandfather Jit
when fathers were the head overseers[29]
the lords were thoughtless
Luang Chom and Grandfather Jit
did wrong with a consort of the palace

---

[24] ศรัทธา, Śarthā. From here, the invocation refers to the myth of the genesis of Nora.

[25] นักเลง, *nakleng*, perhaps here meaning นักแสดง, *nak sadaeng*, performer or expert.

[26] ผมหมอ, *phom mo*, perhaps meaning ผมเอง, *phom eng*, myself, but used later in the invocation to mean an adept, a teacher.

[27] ลุยไฟ, *lui fai*, walking over fire as an ordeal, another courtier in the story. The two named in this line were courtiers who helped Nang Nual Thong Samli; see the myth of the genesis of Nora.

[28] กาศ, *kat*, from ประกาศ, *prakat*.

[29] หลวงนาย, *luang nai*, an overseer or master in charge of men, here probably meaning senior nobles.

and the king ordered they be hanged to death.

fathers had no time to say farewell

no merit to say farewell to their wives

the king ordered they be hanged to death

on the bank of the long river

if fathers had died from sickness

beloved children could ask for news

on the bank of the long river

fathers' lives passed away

fathers died on the bank

to be prey for birds and crows

fathers went to die in the north

let the foul fluids[30] wash down

to dissolve sandal powder[31]

to dissolve powder in oil[32] for anointing

the hard bone, leg bone

we children keep to make phials,[33] eye's jewel,[34]

father Thong Phom Sot[35]

we children will keep to make phials[36] to make hairpins

to admire in place of precious[37] fathers

oh, precious fathers twin jewels,[38] precious fathers

give us your precious love

fathers, do not kill off your love

---

[30] น้ำเน่าน้ำเหงือ, *nam nao nam nguea*, here meaning fluid from the decomposing corpses.

[31] จันทร์ (properly จันทน์), *jan*, a name for several fragrant woods, including sandal, used to make fragrant paste used as a cosmetic and in worship.

[32] Probably here meaning spirit oil, fluid from a corpse used in supernaturalism.

[33] ไม้หลอดอม, *mai lot khom*, meaning a small hollow, usually tubular container to hold fluid materials (mercury, oil) as an amulet; similar to a ปรอท, *phrot*. These amulets are worn to make the Nora singer's voice.

[34] ดวงเนตร, *duang net*, often ดวงเนตา, *duang ta*, literally jewels of the eye, a term of address showing affection.

[35] ทองผมสอด, name of one of the highly revered "royal teachers" of Nora.

[36] ไม้หลอดอม, *mai lot om*.

[37] ร้อยชั่ง, *roi chang*, a hundred of an old monetary denomination worth 80 baht.

[38] สองแถว, *song thaeo*, but more likely สองแก้ว, *song kaeo*, two jewels, another affectionate address.

> do not cut off your children like cutting a palm nut
>
> do not slice us away like slicing banana
>
> fathers, do not squeeze us unto death
>
> have mercy, help us to dance Manohra…

After this invocation, someone in the gathering is usually possessed by one of the ancestral spirits or many of them, or all of them. Usually in each community there is a spirit medium who is well-prepared for this event, but sometimes the ancestral spirits avoid such "preparedness" and choose someone else, immediately after the invocation ends.

The term *Taa-Yaay*, ตา-ยาย, literally means the grandfather and grandmother of the maternal line, in contrast to the terms used for the ancestral spirits of the Northern Thai which is *Phii Puu-Yaa*, ผีปู่ย่า, which means the grandfather and grandmother of the paternal line, and for those of the Northeastern Thai (Isan) which is *Phii Puu-Taa*, ผีปู่ตา, apparently bilateral. The vocabulary used by the Nora seems to retain traces of a matrilineal system and structure within a closed and remote society which is believed to have prevailed among Tai/Thai cultural groups and other Austroasiatic/Austronesian speakers in the distant past when women were the center of communal life and activities, both sexuality and spirituality. Therefore it was the grandmother and the kinswomen of the maternal line who oversaw the behavior of the community including the moral codes, ethics, and values.

Although the Nora lineages of today cannot be traced back into the past to show the intensive practice of matriliny, all Nora ancestral spirits in this *Nora long Khruu* rite appear to be maternal (ตายายโนรา). The 'matri-centered' ritual practice often occurred in most local communities of Southern Thailand as well as in the North, among the Lua of Nan, a Mon-Khmer speaking group in Northern Thailand. (see Cholthira 1998)[39]

Today most celebrated Nora performers are men, including Nora Term (Vin-Vaad) of Trang Province, nevertheless accompanied by women, in this case are Nora Vin and Nora Vaad who happened to be Nora term's wives.

---

[39] Such phenomena also occurred among the Lwa of Chiangmai who practiced matrilineal spirit cults in a very strong sense in the past decades. Although they are now speaking Northern Tai dialect - Kham muang, they were genuinely a Mon-Khmer speaking group or Austroasiatic cultural group by origin. (see Cholthira 1991; 1997; 1998; 2001; 2007)

Nora Ekachai Srivijaya, the celebrity of Nakhon Si Thammarat, and several male Nora performers from Phatthalung are also joined by several female Nora dancers nowadays. However this pattern may not have prevailed in the past, and men may have displaced women at the forefront of Nora quite recently as part of a more widespread transition of gender roles in society. This phenomena may be influenced by the concert of *Phleng Luuk Thung*, เพลงลูกทุ่ง, the popular country music in central and northeastern Thailand, females now feature mostly as backup dancers behind male singing stars, although there are still some exceptions. Yet in some southern Nora communities, both men and women of maternal line still seem to have a dominating role in belief, ritual, and performance.

Nora Saay-Thip of Phatthalung

Nang Saay-Thip Khruea Kaew (โนราสายทิพย์ เครือแก้ว), commonly known as Nora Saay-Thip, is a famous dancer from Phatthalung Province who has performed since childhood and has won fourteen championships in various provinces of Southern Thailand. (www.youtube.com/watch?v=iKjbp-o0Uo8)

Saay-Thip was attracted to Nora from the age of five, and learned from a master as a *khruu phak lak jam* (ครูพัก ลักจำ), an unacknowledged student. Her *maternal uncle* who was a professional Nora performer noticed her talent and gave her encouragement, but her *father* opposed the idea.

According to the story, her father fell sick for unknown reasons and did not respond to *yaa phaaen paccuban* (ยาแผนปัจจุบัน), meaning westernized medicine. Then the father was visited in a dream by her *maternal grandfather*, another Nora master, who advised that he would recover only if he allowed his daughter to become a dancer and continue the Nora practice of their lineage. He consented, recovered and later invested in buying the musical instruments to form a Nora troupe.

The daughter is very appropriately named, *Saay* means a line or lineage, and *thip* comes from a Sanskrit word for a deity, hence "divine lineage" (and also the fruit, nectarine).

Saay-Thip's story tells how a Nora lineage is sustained over time, despite difficulties. It is also significant that the line is passed on from the (spirit of) the maternal grandfather to the daughter, a remnant of *matriliny*.

Nora lineages as a clan system of Southern Thailand
and the Malay periphery

A Nora clan is defined as a group of families or households, the heads of which claim descent from a common ancestor. The whole clan gets together occasionally to perform some ceremony such as the annual ceremony to pay homage to the clan's ancestral spirits.

Strictly speaking, a clan in anthropological terminology is the principal unit of a social organization in which descent is reckoned exclusively through either the paternal or the maternal line. Thus the clansmen and clanswomen are a group of people regarded as being descended from a common ancestor. In the west, the earliest trace of a clan system is usually identified as the Scottish clans of the period 1375-1425 AD. In Asia, clans are found in the early Buddhist Era in India, and during the Hsang Dynasty in China, around five thousand years ago. The Asian records may be legendary, but the *Sākaya Clan* of Lord Buddha may be treated as a historical record.

From my field investigations, I prefer to define the Nora clan system as "a *clandestine lineal administration*."[40] A Nora lineage is a descent group that can demonstrate their common descent from a known apical ancestor. Unilineal lineages may be matrilineal or patrilineal (i.e., traced through mothers or fathers, respectively). Through the course of history, unilineages may transform to become bilateral, or matrilineages may transform into patrilineages, and in some exceptional cases a patrilineage has transformed back into a matrilineage. (Cholthira 1991; Friedman 2002)

Although a clan may claim a common ancestor, often this is a "stipulated descent" that cannot be demonstrated, and sometimes the claimed ancestor is nonhuman and is called a totem. Examples of the clan system in Asia are found in the Chinese, Japanese, Korean, Somali, Miao, Yao, Mon, and Lua/Lawa societies. More than 30 Lua lineages were found in Pua District, Nan Province (Cholthira 1991).

In many Asian and Southeast Asian clan systems, the notion of some common ancestry is loose and unclear, while some clans have their specific totemic motifs, such as, the motif *bird* among the Tai Dam, the *toad* among the Dong, the *dear* among the

---

[40] The general meaning of "clandestine" is something kept secret or done secretively, such as surreptitious or undercover activities. I chose this term because of its deep-rooted semiology (the secret = destined by clan).

Lue, the turtle and swan among the Mon, and the snake, frog, and *buffalo horn* among the Wa of Yunnan evidenced by the Yunnan Bronze Drums. (Cholthira 1991)

To the best of my knowledge, no clan system is found among Thai groups in modern Thailand nowadays. However, the Nora lineages in Southern Thailand today may be the vestiges of a clan system in the past. According to their belief, each lineage has its own ancestral spirits, both male and female.

Originally, the Nora clans were probably matrilineal, but over time became patrilineal or bilateral. Nevertheless there remain indications that the matriline maintains its authority, as in the Saay-Thip case outlined above, and elsewhere.

In February 2013, I conducted another anthropological fieldwork among Thai communities across the border in rural areas of Kedah state of Malaysia on the speculation that old practices and identities may have become frozen when the communities were isolated in a culturally alien environment. Although I did not have any expectations of this fieldwork, I was pleasantly surprised.(Appadurai 1988, Bhabha 1994)

Mae Hmoe Nual is a single woman of Saiburi (ไทรบุรี, Kedah) from a Tai-speaking group who call themselves *Chao Siam* (ชาวสยาม), or *Orang Siam*. Speaking in Thai, which she called *bhāsā siam*, she related that her grandmother's family was from around Phatthalung/Songkhla, her mother had been born in Saiburi under British colonial rule, and her father came from Southern Thailand (perhaps Songkhla/Nakhon Si Thammarat). She lives among relatives who share a belief in worshipping an ancestral totem in the form of crocodiles, known as Taa Khee (ตา เข้ , it is the motif of *jorakhee*, จระเข้).[41]

Her (maternal) grandmother (ยาย) had impressed upon Nual, her elder brother, and their maternal cousins the importance of upholding traditional "Siamese" values in the nontraditional setting of rural Malaysia. She was taught at an early age the importance of family ties and ancestry, of sharing food and work, of listening to children and elders, of showing respect to all people whether human or animal, and in particular showing high respect towards the Taa Khee. Nual did not like dancing and could not dance, but she was the *"chosen one"* of Taa Khee, who transformed her and worked with her in

---

[41] Thanks Oliver Raendchen [SEACOM, Berlin] who led me to meet Mae Hmoe Nual in Kedah, and hinted me on her specific belief in totemic motif – the *crocodiles.*

the annual ceremony when all members of the same (clan) belief system gathered to pay homage and respects to the ancestral spirits. Nual had thus become known as Mae Hmoe Nual, mother-adept Nual, a mix of shamaness and spirit-medium, respected not only by her relatives of the same clan, but also by almost the whole community including peoples of other villages. Among her services were fortune-telling and healing with sacred water and traditional herbs.

The prayers and sermon spoken at this ceremony emerged from her memory, passed down to her by the ancestors, sensed only dimly until they emerged under spirit-possession.

She said she was inspired by stories of transformation told by her (maternal) grandmother. While she was possessed, the ancestors transformed themselves into her, and brought her closer to their ways of knowing persons, relatives, offspring, and village life. She was stirred by the ritual offerings and atmosphere of traditional belief. Her spiritual mind explored stories from the ancient past and their interplay, confluence and divergence, with her everyday life. Possession by the *Taa Khee* was both a physical as well as a spiritual experience for her. When the ancestral spirits took hold of her, she felt overjoyed, and when they left her, she felt relieved and fulfilled. After each occasion she felt unwilling to repeat the experience, but was helpless as she was chosen and gradually became more familiar with the experience. The faces of the ancestors reminded her of their resilient animal body, their inborn ability to greet the good stories of their life with pleasure and their dark stories with courage and personal transformation.

There appear to be various layers of belief involved here. The belief in the crocodile ancestral spirits appears to be the oldest layer, a remnant of an ancient clan system. Within her extended family, there are two lineages which maintained the Nora rituals and performance. Although Nual herself could not dance, she was chosen and possessed by her maternal ancestors, *Taa Khee*, to pass down the knowledge, wisdom, and moral code of the clan for posterity. (see Baker 1999, *"Divine Inspiration"-The case in Latin America*)

The clan ritual was closely associated with veneration of the dead, based on a belief that the deceased have a continued existence and possess the ability to influence the fortune of the living. The goal of ancestor veneration is to ensure the ancestors' continued well-being and positive disposition towards the living and sometimes to ask for special favors or assistance.

The social function of ancestor veneration is to cultivate kinship values, such as family loyalty, kinship bond, and continuity of the family lineage. Ancestor veneration occurs in societies with differing degree of social, political, and technological complexity, and remains an important component of various religious practices in modern times.

Pithī Long Khruu Nora and the veneration of the dead

The minimum requirement for venerating the dead is a belief in the survival of personal identity for some period beyond death, without expectation of an afterlife. If the dead are not properly venerated, there is risk of some misfortune, including death, befalling the surviving members of the same clan.

The Nora ancestry practices differ from worshipping a deity or the Buddha at a home or temple in order to ask for some favor. The veneration of ancestors is a filial duty, undertaken because the ancestors need help from their descendants, because expression of filial piety is important, and because the ancestors receive what is offered when the rite is properly performed. The act is a way to respect, honor, and look after ancestors in their afterlives as well as a way to seek guidance for their living descendants.

In this regard, the Nora culture and the veneration of ancestors overlap. The Nora dance and rituals are equivalent to prayers offered to honor the clan ancestors and to ask for their continued assistance for their living descendants. However, maintaining the Nora practices is not only a form of worship but also an imperative duty to preserve the Nora ritual performance for the future.

Why is this so significant?

Because the Nora ritual performance is a symbolic cultural survival of the clan system.

Pithī Long Khruu Nora is an occasion to celebrate the beloved Nora ancestors, reunite members of the same Nora clan and community, and all enjoy a festive atmosphere. Residents of surrounding villages are often invited to attend the veneration, where food and liquor are typically served and a Nora troupe or more performs.

Veneration of ancestors is also demonstrated through adherence to taboos that are respected beyond the lifetime of the ancestor who established them. Misfortunes are often attributed to ancestors whose memory or wishes have been neglected. Sacrificial offerings of chicken, pig or even cow/buffalo together with betel nuts and liquor are a traditional method used to appease and honor the ancestors.

The term 'Nora' and the 'Herstory of Manohara'

Nora is generally believed to be an abbreviated form of *Manohara*. The story of Manohra or Nora comes from a tale about a *kinarī* (นางกินรี), a woman-bird figure who lives in the Himavanta forest.

The tale appears in the *Divyavadana* (ทิพยวทาน), meaning "divine story-telling" in Sanskrit, an anthology of Buddhist tales probably dating to the 2nd century AD, and was depicted in many ancient monuments including stone reliefs at Borobodur in Indonesia. The story has been well-known in Cambodia, Thailand, and Indonesia, including among the local communities of the Dai/Tai speaking groups in South and Southwestern China, particularly in the Tai-Yunnan periphery.

The *Paññāsa-jātaka* (ปัญญาสชาดก), a Pali collection of *jataka* tales written by a Buddhist monk in Chiang Mai around 1450-1470 AD, included the story. There are similar versions told in China, Japan and Korea, including the Chinese story of the Princess and the Cowherd.

These various stories share a basic plot but with many variations.

In the version best known in Thailand, there are *seven* winged princesses or *kinarī*, daughters of Phraya Kinara, who live on Mount Krailaś in Himavanta. One day they fly down to earth in order to take a bath. The youngest and prettiest, *the "Seventh" princess* - Manohara, is captured by a human hunter (พรานบุญ), who presents her to a prince, Phra Sudhana (พระสุธน), who falls in love with her and marries her. Later in the story, while the prince is away at war, misfortune befalls the city and Manohara is blamed for bringing bad luck and is threatened with death. She dons her wings, transforming herself back into a *kinarī*, and flies back to her native heavenly forest, leaving behind a ring and a clue so that Prince Sudhana may search for her.

On return from war, Phra Sudhana lives on a long and adventurous journey of pursuit, and faces many tests of his strength, perseverance, wit and wisdom before he can find Manohara and they may live happily ever after.

Although other stories are performed with Nora performance technique, the story of Manohara is considered the original and also the most attractive, with many appealing touches, such as the depiction of the forest hunter as a comic personality of lower social status.

Here I would like to emphasize that Nora or Manohara is a story with a heroine as its focus. It is not a *his-story* of Phra Sudhana, but a *her-story* of Manohara, who lives across the span of the heavenly and human worlds. Amazingly, she happened to be "the Seventh". (The belief in the magic and misfortune of someone who were "the Seventh" will be further studied and elaborated in terms of cross-cultural study in the next volume of this Series by the same researcher.)

Her home is the sacred space of Himavanta, a heavenly domain full of mythical and divine figures. She can fly down to earth and fly high up to the sky. She can transform herself to live either in the human world or heaven. Neither the man-hunter nor the human prince has such talents. Without her, there would be no story, no beginning, no end.

She is the *creatress* of the Nora story.

This *her-story* has been retold from place to place, from time to time, across Southeast Asia, India, China, Korea, and Japan.

It is a basic element of the cultural space and the social system of the Tai/Thai/Siam culture with Austroasiatic and Austronesian connections, having the *kinarī* figure as semiotic totem of the Nora clan. *Totemism* is a system of belief closely attached with the clan system in which each human social organization is thought to have a spiritual connection or kinship with a physical being, such as an animal or plant, often called a spirit-being or totem. The totem is thought to interact with the kin group or individual and serves as their emblem or symbol.[42] The the *kinarī* figure is undoubtedly the totem of several clannish communities of Southern Thailand, including some Siamese indigenous communities in Kelantan, Tranganoo, Kedah, and Perlis who are Tai speaking ethnical groups across the border of Thailand and Malaysia.

---

[42] The term *totem* is derived from the Ojibwa word *ototeman*, meaning "one's brother-sister kin." The grammatical root, *ote*, signifies a blood relationship between brothers and sisters who have the same mother and who may not marry each other.

In English, the word *"totem"* was introduced in 1791 by a British merchant and translator who gave it a false meaning in the belief that it designated the guardian spirit of an individual, who appeared in the form of an animal—an idea that the Ojibwa clans did indeed portray by their wearing of animal skins. It was reported at the end of the 18th century that the Ojibwa named their clans after those animals that live in the area in which they live and appear to be either friendly or fearful. The first accurate report about *totemism* in North America was written by a Methodist missionary, Peter Jones, himself an Ojibwa, who died in 1856 and whose report was published posthumously. According to Jones, the Great Spirit had given *toodaims* (totems) to the Ojibwa clans, and because of this act, members of the group are related to one another and on this account may not marry among themselves.

An open-ended conclusion

Traditional ritual and performing arts are indicators of traditional knowledge systems of people once living in remote areas. As James D. Wolfensohn, former president of the World Bank, said,

> The indigenous knowledge is an integral part of the culture and history of a local community. We need to learn from local communities to enrich the development process. (Gorjestani 2000)

There is enormous scope to document the traditional knowledge systems still prevailing in Southern Thailand and adjacent areas of Malaysia before they disappear into oblivion in this age of globalization. My discussion outlines the active interaction of people living with the natural environment through sustainable ecological resources of the surrounding environment, reflecting traditional knowledge systems generated through a long period of time.

Today, the wisdom of Nora still has a function within localities where the Nora clan system and lineages exist. But amidst the economic, social and cultural changes of consumerism and globalization, Nora performance may lose its power and authority in the years to come.

In social science research, the south has remained the least explored region of Thailand. Despite its turbulent past of several decades of communist guerilla warfare, followed by outbreaks of "terrorism" and "separatism," Southern Thailand still maintains a spirit of harmony. The communities associated with the Nora clans and lineages[43] have contributed to this spirit, to the development of unity in diversity, and to the preservation of cultural survivals for the long term.

The Nora clan system has deep roots in the culture of Southern Thailand. It was originally based around matrilineal ancestral spirit cults, expressed in forms of ritual and dramatic performance, with different taboos and totems in different areas.

In recent years of modernization, most Nora lineages have been taken over by males who can perform both dance and supernaturalism (คุณไสย, *khun sai*). They have converted Nora to serve their own needs with the help of Brahmanism and Buddhism.

---

[43] There is also some kind of clan system and lineage associated with the puppet performance, *nang talung* (หนังตะลุง). This is not the topic of my research, but it is strongly recommended for others to explore in anthropological perspective.

They sometimes abuse the wisdom of Nora for economic purpose, turning rituals into commodities.

Some female Nora practitioners have offered resistance by maintaining maternal ancestral spirit cults and preserving secret knowledge. These maternal lineages have revived women's power, wisdom, and art and have been able to establish their authority in some rural communities of the three provinces.

The Nora lineages of today probably developed from an indigenous clan system, whose skill and wisdom, both *Śāstra* (sciences) and *Śilapa* (art), have deep historic and religious roots with the Austroasiatic/Austronesian connections. This clan system was modified through the long course of history of Southeast Asia and the Malay peninsula under the influence of Brahmanism, Buddhism, and male ambitions. Nevertheless women have maintained their power within the hidden structure of the Nora clans/lineages, and function as the loyal guardians of ethical values among the younger generations in local communities, colleges, and universities until today.

References

Books and Journals in English

Appadurai, A.

    1988 *"Putting Hierarchy in Its Place," Cultural Anthropology* 3(1): 36-49.

Baker, Carol Anne

    1999 *"Divine Inspiration," MACLAS, Latin American Essays,* Vol. XIII, Middle Atlantic for Latin American Studies, March 1999, ©2000 by MACLAS, 47-62 pp.

Baudrillard, Jean

    1998 *The Consumer Society : Myths and Structures,* Sage Publications Ltd.

Bhabha, Homi

    1994 *The Location of Culture.* New York: Routledge.

Boul, Augusto

    1979 *Theatre of the Oppressed,* translated by Charles A. and Maria-Odilia Leal McBride, Theatre Communications Group Inc., New York: Urizen Books.

Chesneaux, Jean

    1992 *Brave Modern World : The Prospects For Survival,* Thames & Hudson.

Cholthira Satyawadhna

    1991 *"The Dispossessed: An Anthropological Reconstruction of Lawa Ethnohistory in the Light of Their Relationship with the Tai,"* Ph.D. thesis, submitted to The Australian National University.

    1997 *"Ethnic Inter-relationships in the History of Lanna: Reconsidering the Lwa Role in the Lanna Scenario",* in *TAI CULTURE, International Review on Tai Cultural Studies.* Vol.II, No.2, December 1997: pp. 6-29. 1997.

    1998 *"Folk Wisdom, Spirit Cults, and Power Change of the Lua and Muang at the Boe Kluea Salt Mine of Nan Province",* in *TAI CULTURE, International Review on Tai Cultural Studies.* Vol.III, No.1 , June 1998: pp. 121-142. [Research paper presented in the International Conference on "Spirit Cults in Southeast asia" at the Museum of Ethnology, Osaka, in1992]

    2001 *"Appropriation of Women's Indigenous Knowledge: The Case of the Matrilineal Lua in Northern Thailand,"* Gender Technology and Development, Vol.5, No.1, January-April 2001: pp.91-111. 2001, Asian Institute of Technology, Thailand.

2007 *"The Feminine Time and Women's Space",* Special Issue on Women and Gender in Tai Societies, TAI CULTURE, International Review on Tai Cultural Studies. Vol.19, No.1, January 2007: 5-11. Center of Thai-Asian Studies, Rangsit University, Pathumthani, Thailand, in collaboration with South East Asian Communication Centre [SEACOM], Berlin, Germany.

Dumont, Louise

©1971 *Homo hierarchicus. Essai sur le système des castes,* Paris, Gallimard.

Homo hierarchicus : The Caste System and Its Implications, University of Chicago Press, 1977, reprint 1981.

©1977 *Homo aequalis: genèse et épanouissement de l'idéologie économique,* Paris, Gallimard, reprint 1991.

Friedman, Jonathan

2002 *"From Roots to Routes – Tropes for Trippers,"* Anthropological Theory. London: Sage Publication.

Geertz, Clifford

1973 *Old Societies and New States* (1963), reprinted in *The Interpretation of Cultures.* New York: Basic Books Inc.

1981 *Negara: The Theatre State in Nineteenth-Century Bali.* Princeton: Princeton University Press.

2000 *"The World in Pieces: Culture and Politics at the End of the Century,"* in *Available Light: Anthropological Reflections on Philosophical Topics.* Princeton: Princeton University Press.

Gorjestani, Nicolas

2000 *"Indigenous Knowledge for Development: Opportunities and Challenges,"* Indigenous Knowledge for Development Program, The World Bank. (Paper presented for the UNCTAD Conference on Traditional Knowledge in Geneva, November 2000.)

Harner, Michael

©1998 *My Path in Shamanism - Interview with Michael Harner,* in Roger Walsh and Charles S. Grob (Eds.), *Higher Wisdom.* Albany: State University of New York Press, 2005.

Horrigan, Bonnie

1997 *"Shamanic Healing: We Are Not Alone,"* An Interview of Michael Harner by Bonnie Horrigan. Shamanism, Spring/Summer 1997, Vol. 10, No. 1: 1-4.

Scott, James C.

1987 *Weapons of the Weak: Everyday Forms of Resistance*, New Haven, Conn.: Yale University Press.

Shiva, Vandana

1989 *Staying Alive: Women, Ecology and Development,* London: Zed Books.

Sullivan, Lawrence E.

1994 *"The Attributes and Power of the Shaman: A General Description of the Estatic Care of the Soul"* in Jane S. Day and Gary Seaman (Eds.), *Ancient Traditions: Shamanism in Central Asia and the Americas.* Niwot: U.P. Colorado.

Books in Thai

Chatthip Nartsupha and Pornpilai Lertwicha

2541 *"Southern Thailand – The Ancestral spirits rite,"* in *wadhnadham mooban thai* [Thai Villages Cultures]. Bangkok: Sangsun Books, pp. 132-137.

Chawalit Angwitayadhorn

2553 *"Nakhon-Lakhon (นคร-ลคร – The land of Manohara"* in *amlaa aalay naay Chawalit Angwitayadhorn* [In Memory of Mr. Chawalit Angwitayadhorn]. Nakhon Si Thammarat: Wat Chamao, pp.29-30.

Prateep Chumphol

2546 *"Bot Nora"*(บทโนรา) and *"Manohara Nibat lae Manora"* (มโนหรานิบาต และ มโนรา) in *Phinit Wannakam Phak Tai* (Critique on Southern Thai Literature). Bangkok: Nam Fon Publishing House, pp. 23-24; 137-142.

Wanida Chumnum

2554 *"Nora"*(โนรา) in *Nora - Kalau* (โนรา – กาหลอ), edited by Suebpong Thammachart. Nakhon Si Thammarat: Walailak Cultural Aśram (อาศรมวัฒนธรรมวลัยลักษณ์), Walailak University, pp. 9-87.

Information retrieved from Cyber Space

http://www.shamanism.org/index.php, retrieved May-June 2013.
http://www.shamanism.org/articles/article01.html, retrieved May-June 2013.
http://www.worldbank.org/afr/ik/ikpaper_0102.pdf, retrieved March 2013.
http://krunora.blogspot.com/2013/05/blog-post_13.html, retrieved January-June 2013.

Ritual Performance of Southeast Asia   Volume II

ANTHROPOLOGY OF SOUTHEAST ASIA

The Ritual Performance of SEA Series

The Ritual Performance of SEA Series shows the exposition of both rituals and dances of Southeast Asia in anthropological perspectives.

Volume II

Cholthira Satyawadhna[*]

HERSTORY: MANOHARA
The Archetype of the 'Seventh Daughter' in Southern Thai, Malaysia, and European Myths

In Volume II, a cross-cultural study in anthropological perspective is further conducted in order to show that there has been some significant linkage in the belief of the magic of "the Seventh" within the Thai, Southeast Asian, and European myths.

---

[*]   **Cholthira Satyawadhna**
B.A., M.A. in Thai Language and Literature (Chulalongkorn University);
Ph.D. in Anthropology (The Australian National University)

Academic Profile
Professeur des Universités in Thai and Asian Studies, ISCID, Université du Littorale, Academie de Lille, France;
Senior Researcher in Social Sciences and Humanities, Rangsit University, Thailand;
Supervisor, Doctoral Program in Asian Studies, School of Liberal Arts, Walailak University; Southern Thailand;
Radcliffe Fellow, Radcliffe Institute for Advanced Study, Harvard University, USA.